Move Adventures

UNDERSEA EDITION

A children's interactive musical and movement activity book

By Samantha Macino

Canton, Ohio, USA

Macino Book Adventures, LLC

Written and digitally illustrated by
Samantha Macino

First edition

ISBN: 978-1-971759-01-2

Library of Congress Control Number: 2026903079

Disclaimer
This book is intended for educational and entertainment purposes only. The movement and activity suggestions are designed for young children and should be completed with appropriate adult supervision. Always ensure activities are performed in a safe space suitable for children.

This Book Belongs To:

_____

_____

Parents & Caregivers

This book is designed to help young children move, listen, and play while exploring rain forest animals. Each page invites
your child to copy a simple movement and sound, building body awareness, confidence, and joy through active participation.

Tips When Reading This Book

- Read it out loud and encourage your child to move along.
- Model the movements, children love copying grown-ups!
- Repeat chants as many times as your child wants.
- It's okay if movements look different. There is no "right" way to move.
- Follow your child's lead. Some children may jump and roar. Others may watch, sway, or make quiet sounds. All responses are valid and meaningful.

Welcome, to under the sea,
Where songs and splashes wait for thee!
Stretch your arms and wiggle free,
It's time to move-come swim with me!

Turtle takes a quiet ride,
Arms move wide from side to side.
Paddle left and paddle right,
Breathe in deep, breathe out light.
Turtle swims-calm and sturdy.
Slow and steady, don't you hurry!

Did You Know?
Sea turtles use their strong flippers to swim very far-flap your arms slow and wide like a turtle!

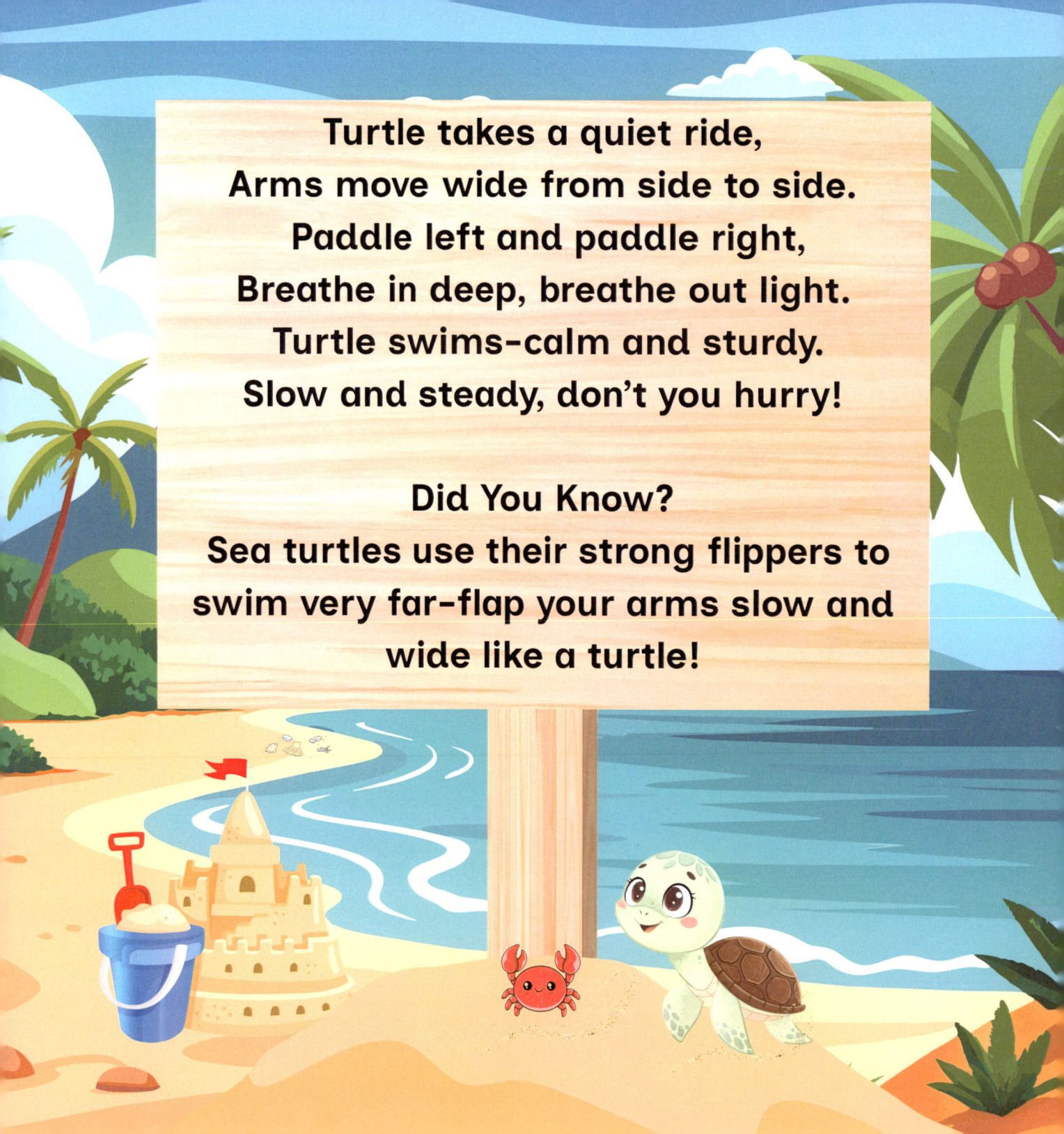

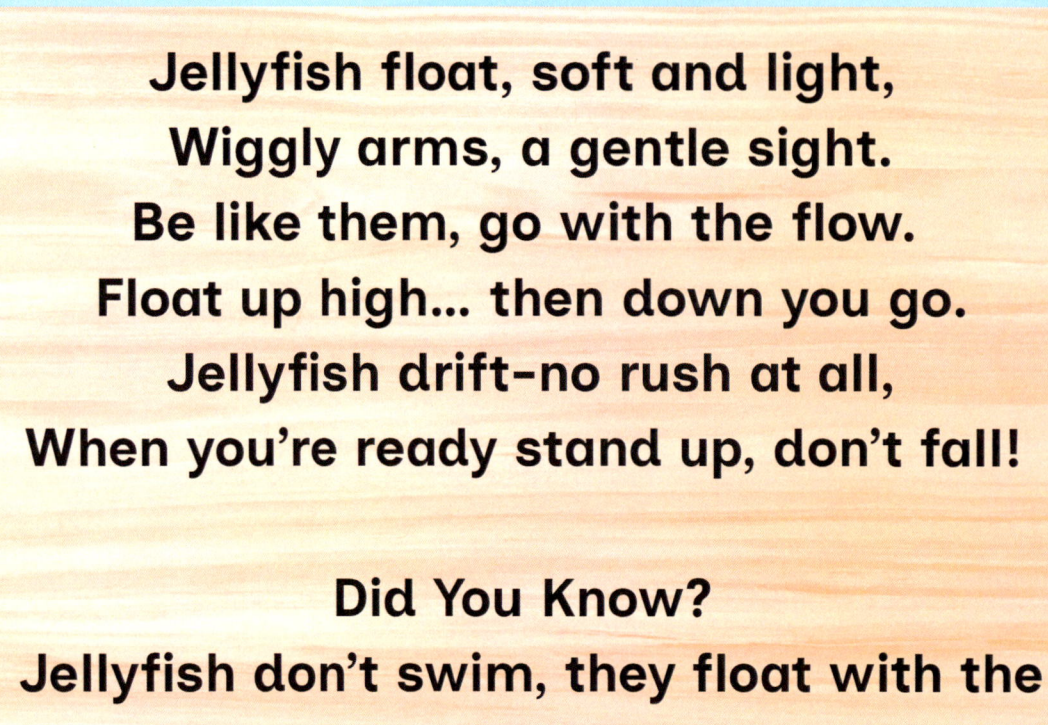

Jellyfish float, soft and light,
Wiggly arms, a gentle sight.
Be like them, go with the flow.
Float up high... then down you go.
Jellyfish drift-no rush at all,
When you're ready stand up, don't fall!

Did You Know?
Jellyfish don't swim, they float with the
ocean currents.
Raise your arms, sway softly, float up
high... then gently drift down.

Starfish stretch so big and wide,
Reach for waves on every side.
Stretch out wide just like a star,
Five-point sparkle, here you are!
Starfish sparkle beneath the bay,
Hold it still, don't tip or sway.

Did You Know?
Starfish can grow back their arms - stretch your arms wide and hold them strong!

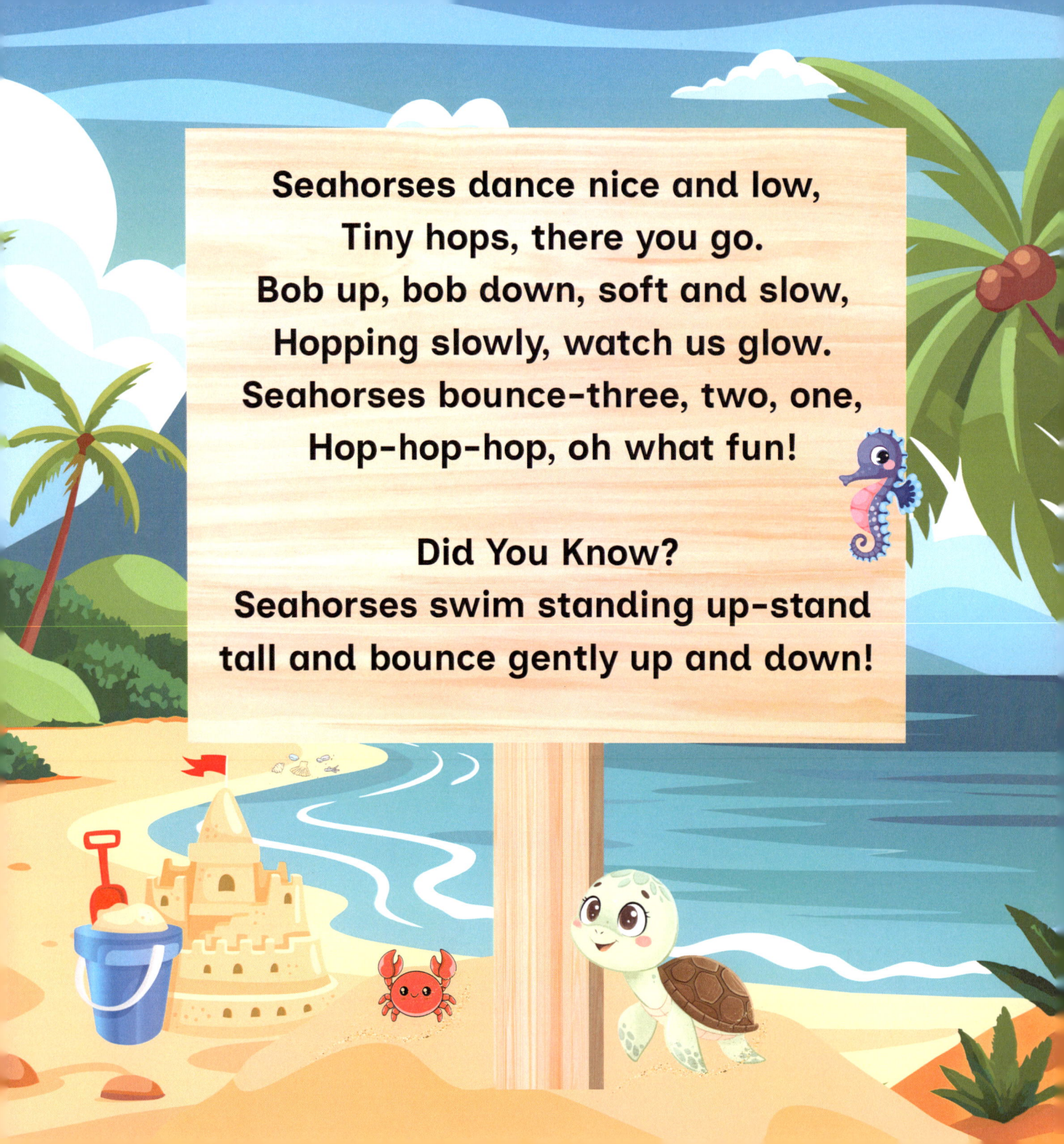

Seahorses dance nice and low,
Tiny hops, there you go.
Bob up, bob down, soft and slow,
Hopping slowly, watch us glow.
Seahorses bounce-three, two, one,
Hop-hop-hop, oh what fun!

Did You Know?
Seahorses swim standing up-stand
tall and bounce gently up and down!

Swish-swish-swim, little fish,
Fast or slow, make a wish!
Zoom ahead, then turn around,
Through the bubbles, up and down!
Fishy friends, come splash around,
Swish your tail and spin around!

Did You Know?
Fish wiggle their tails to move through
the water-swish your hips side to side
like a fish!

Dolphin jumps, up so high!
Click-click-clap, as you fly!
Splash back down, splash-ker-splat!
Hear that sound, imagine that!
Dolphin dance, here we go!
Click-click-clap, go, go, go!

Did You Know?
Dolphins jump out of the water when they're happy-jump up high and splash back down!

Whale goes whoosh with mighty waves,
Stomp-stomp-splash through ocean caves.
Big blue whale goes down, down, down,
Splashy tail-turn around!
Take deep breaths-blow up high!
Whale songs fill the sea and sky!

Did You Know?
Whales take big breaths through their blowholes-take a deep breath in and blow it out high!

Eight arms wiggle, count them all!
Shake them big, shake them small!
Shake them silly, wild and free!
Twist, bend, and wobble in the sea!
Wiggle, wobble, round and round,
Octopus fun-make a sound!

Did You Know?
Octopuses have eight arms that can
twist and bend-wiggle all eight arms
any way you want!

Manta ray glides smooth and wide,
Floating through the ocean tide.
Arms like wings-stretch and sway,
Drift so high along the bay.
Manta ray flies through the sea,
Quiet, calm, and graceful as can be.

Did You Know?
Manta rays glide like they're flying-
stretch your arms wide and float around
the room!

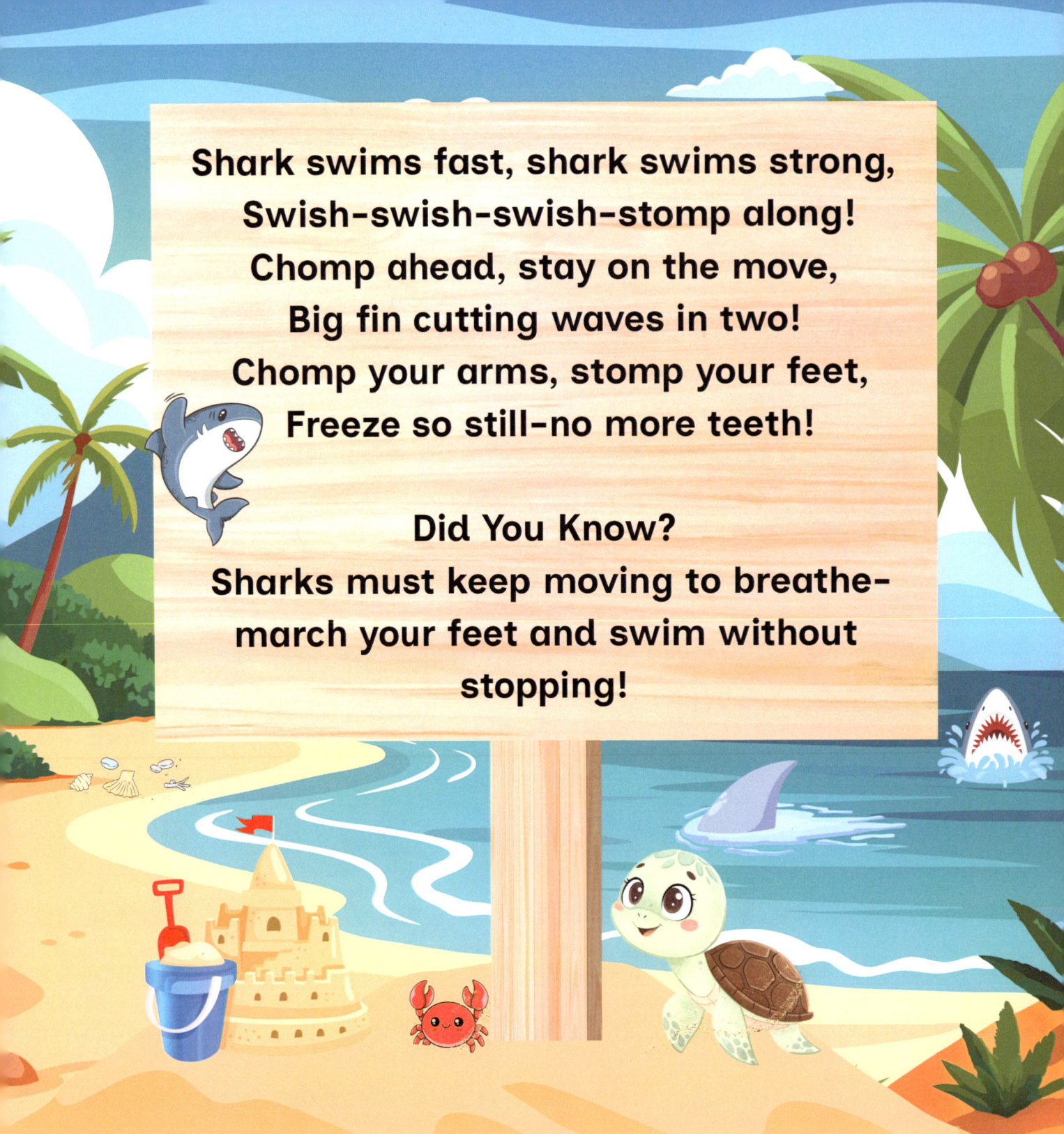

Shark swims fast, shark swims strong,
Swish-swish-swish-stomp along!
Chomp ahead, stay on the move,
Big fin cutting waves in two!
Chomp your arms, stomp your feet,
Freeze so still-no more teeth!

Did You Know?
Sharks must keep moving to breathe-
march your feet and swim without
stopping!

Thank you boys and girls, that's the end.
Moving is fun, let's do this again!

Samantha Macino is a children's book author, digital designer, and psychiatric nurse practitioner with a master's degree in nursing. She works with children and adolescents in high-need community settings, where she supports mental health, development, and family connection. As a mother of four, Samantha understands the importance of movement, play, and meaningful interaction in early childhood. Her books are thoughtfully designed to help caregivers engage with children while promoting physical activity, emotional well-being, and developmental growth. Writing allows Samantha to combine her clinical knowledge with her passion for creativity, giving purpose to her work both professionally and personally.

If you liked this book, please check out my other work!

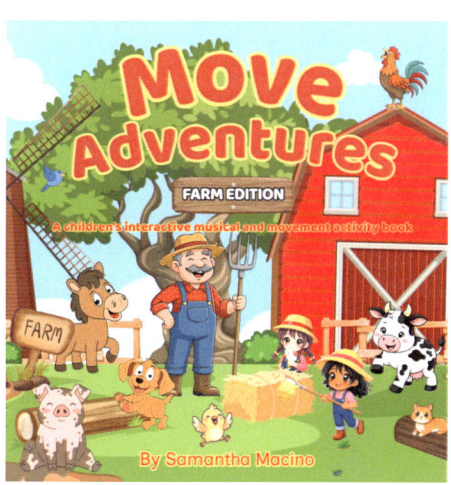
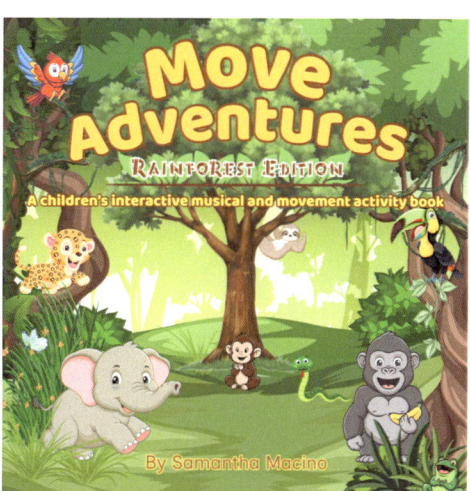
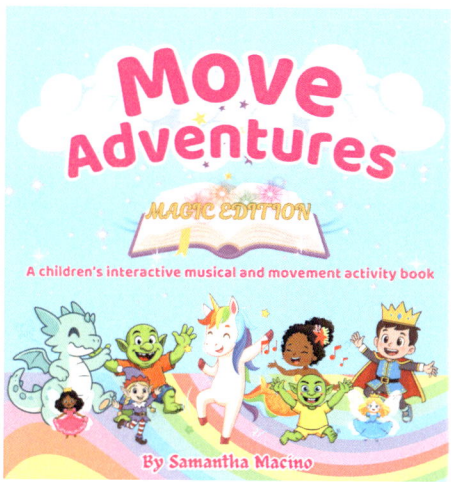

If you enjoyed this book, please leave a review online!

Macino Book Adventures, LLC
Macinobookadventures.org

Bonus Content: Fun Fats

🐢 Sea Turtle
Did you know? Sea turtles can live to be very old, some over 100 years!

Did you know? Sea turtles use their flippers like wings to fly through the water.

🪼 Jellyfish
Did you know? Jellyfish don't have brains or bones, they're super squishy!

Did you know? Some jellyfish glow in the dark like underwater lights.

⭐ Starfish
Did you know? Starfish have small eye spots on the tip of each arm.

Did you know? Starfish don't have blood, they use seawater to move their bodies.

🐴 Seahorse
Did you know? Seahorses are the slowest swimming fish.

Did you know? Daddy seahorses carry the babies in a special pouch.

🐠 Fish
Did you know? Fish use their fins to turn, stop, and zoom through the water.

Did you know? Fish can sleep with their eyes open.

🐬 Dolphin
Did you know? Dolphins are great jumpers and love to play games.

Did you know? Dolphins talk to each other using clicks and whistles.

🐋 Whale
Did you know? Whales are some of the biggest animals on Earth.

Did you know? A whale's song can travel for miles underwater.

🐙 Octopus
Did you know? Octopuses have three hearts and nine brains.

Did you know? Octopuses can change colors to hide or show how they feel.

🦋 Manta Ray
Did you know? Manta rays flap their fins like birds flying underwater.

Did you know? Manta rays are gentle giants and don't sting.

🦈 Shark
Did you know? Sharks have been swimming in the ocean longer than dinosaurs lived on land.

Did you know? Sharks can smell food from very far away.

Learning Objectives

This book is designed to support early childhood development through music, movement, and imaginative play. As children sing, move, and explore the ocean, they will build important skills in a joyful and engaging way.

Through this book, children will:
- Develop gross motor skills. Practice jumping, stretching, swaying, twisting, balancing, and moving their bodies in new ways.
- Build body awareness and coordination. Learn how different parts of their body move together as they copy animal motions.
- Strengthen listening and following directions. Follow simple movement cues and rhythmic patterns within each song.
- Support early language development. Hear repeated rhymes, action words, and animal vocabulary to encourage speech and comprehension.
- Encourage creativity and imagination. Pretend to move like sea animals while exploring rhythm, expression, and playful storytelling.
- Learn fun ocean facts through movement. Connect simple animal facts with physical actions to help information "stick" through the body.
- Promote joyful, screen-free learning. Turn story time into active play at home, in classrooms, or during group activities.